30 SHORT BEDTIME STORIES FOR KIDS

BASED ON ISLAMIC VALUES FOR MUSLIM CHILDREN

SCAN QR CODE WITH YOUR PHONE TO VIEW ALL OUR BOOKS

PUBLISHED BY

JOLLY MUSLIM
.COM

COPYRIGHT © 2024
ALL RIGHTS RESERVED
JOLLY MUSLIM PUBLISHING

WWW.JOLLYMUSLIM.COM

CONTENTS PAGE

VALUE 1: GOD-CONSCIOUSNESS
ALI'S AMAZING ADVENTURE — 5

VALUE 2: SINCERITY
AMINA'S KINDNESS QUEST — 7

VALUE 3: HONESTY
AHMED AND THE LOST KITE — 9

VALUE 4: INTEGRITY
FATIMA'S FAIR PLAY — 11

VALUE 5: GRATITUDE
YOUSSEF'S THANKFUL TREE — 13

VALUE 6: PATIENCE
LAYLA'S ENCHANTED GARDEN — 15

VALUE 7: HUMILITY
OMAR'S HUMBLE PIE — 17

VALUE 8: RESPECT FOR PARENTS
AYESHA'S SECRET SURPRISE — 19

VALUE 9: KINDNESS
KHALID'S KINDNESS CREW — 21

VALUE 10: GENEROSITY
NADIA'S SHARING PICNIC — 23

CONTENTS PAGE

VALUE 11: FORGIVENESS
ELIAS AND THE FRIENDSHIP FORGIVENESS — 25

VALUE 12: GOOD MANNERS
SARA'S SWEET WORDS — 27

VALUE 13: DIGNITY
ZAINAB'S STAND FOR JUSTICE — 29

VALUE 14: LOYALTY
AMIN AND THE FRIENDSHIP TREE — 31

VALUE 15: RESPECT FOR ELDERS
GRANDMA'S TEA PARTY — 33

VALUE 16: RESPONSIBILITY
HANA'S RESPONSIBLE RABBIT — 35

VALUE 17: CLEANLINESS
ADAM'S CLEAN-UP ADVENTURE — 37

VALUE 18: CONTENTMENT
KAMRAN'S SIMPLE TREASURES — 39

VALUE 19: COURAGE
KARIM'S BRAVE QUEST — 41

VALUE 20: OPTIMISM
FARAH'S DAY OF HAPPINESS — 43

CONTENTS PAGE

VALUE 21: MODESTY
Jamal's Modesty Show — 45

VALUE 22: TRUTHFULNESS
Zara's Truth Telling Adventure — 47

VALUE 23: SELF DISCIPLINE
Rayan's Self-Discipline Superpower — 49

VALUE 24: ENVIRONMENTAL PROTECTION
Sadia and the Green Team — 51

VALUE 25: FRIENDSHIP
Tahir's Unbreakable Bond — 53

VALUE 26: KNOWLEDGE SEEKING
Nora's Quest for Knowledge — 55

VALUE 27: PURITY OF HEART
Zayn's Pure Heart — 57

VALUE 28: DUA
Zeeshan's Prayer Beads — 59

VALUE 29: GRACIOUSNESS
Hiba's Act of Grace — 61

VALUE 30: TOLERANCE
Lina's Cultural Acceptance — 63

VALUE 1: GOD-CONSCIOUSNESS

ALI'S AMAZING ADVENTURE

Once upon a time, in a happy little town, there was a boy named Ali who loved to go on adventures. He heard a secret about a hidden treasure! Ali's eyes widened with delight, and he was determined to embark on an adventure to find it.

Ali set out on a journey through forests, across rivers, and over large mountains, armed with an old map he discovered in a dusty book. But his journey was not without challenges. Along the way, he faced difficult challenges that put his courage and honesty to the test.

Ali came across a bird with a broken wing one day. He wanted to help, but he was eager to find the treasure quickly. Then he thought to himself that helping the bird would make Allah happy. Ali listened to his inner thoughts, and made a small splint for the bird. The bird was now able to fly again!

Ali kept on his journey and felt happy inside.

As Ali continued, he came across a dragon guarding a sparkling bridge. The dragon appeared frightening, but Ali knew that Allah was more stronger than a dragon. With confidence, Ali approached the dragon and to his surprise it spoke gently. It told stories about being truthful and honest. Ali realised that honesty was just as important as bravery. So he told the dragon about his quest, and the dragon allowed him to safely cross the river.

Ali learned something special called God-consciousness through all of his adventures. It meant making decisions that pleased Allah. Ali realised that the true treasure was not gold or jewels. It was having a heart filled with God-consciousness — being kind, helping others, and making wise decisions.

Ali discovered a glowing light in the middle of a magical forest. The light shone brighter when he opened his heart to Allah and chose to do good. It brought joy and warmth to the forest. Ali realised that the best treasure was a sense of peace, gratitude, and closeness to Allah.

When Ali returned to his hometown, he didn't have gold, but he did have something better. He had stories about being kind, brave, and making wise decisions. Ali's adventure became well-known, and local children were inspired to emulate him. They discovered that the most valuable treasures can be found in our hearts.

So Ali's story lived on in the happy little town, reminding everyone that the best adventures are the ones in which we make Allah happy and fill our hearts with goodness.

VALUE 2: SINCERITY

AMINA'S KINDNESS QUEST

A little girl named Amina lived in a cheerful town where giggles and sunshine filled the air. Amina had a sun-warming heart and a smile that could brighten even the darkest day. She enjoyed making people happy and decided to embark on a special adventure one day.

Amina's journey was not about discovering hidden treasures or magical lands. No, her mission was to spread kindness like seeds, causing her town to bloom with joy. Amina's genuine desire to please Allah was what made her kindness quest truly extraordinary.

Amina set out on her journey with a basket full of smiles and a pocket full of giggles. Mrs. Johnson's house was her first stop, and she offered to help with the garden. Mrs. Johnson watched, surprised and delighted, as Amina watered the flowers and weeded the garden with a joyful heart.

Amina then went to the playground, where she noticed a shy girl sitting alone. She greeted her with a cheerful "Hello!" and they were soon swinging and laughing together. Amina's generosity extended beyond grand gestures to make every moment special for someone else.

Amina's acts of kindness increased as she skipped through town. She helped Mr. Patel carry groceries, shared her favourite toy with Sara, her younger friend, and even left encouraging notes on people's doors. Amina's heart was overflowing with joy as she spread kindness.

Amina's quest was truly unique because of her secret ingredient, sincerity. It was like a bright light in her heart that guided every kind act. Amina wasn't being nice just to be noticed; she was doing it to make Allah happy. This made her kindness pure and unique, as if it were a hidden gift from the universe.

Amina realised something magical one day while sitting under the big oak tree. The real treasures were the joy she felt from helping others, the smiles she shared, and the warmth in her heart. It wasn't about what she got, but about the joy she brought to others.

Amina's quest for kindness did not come to an end. It turned into a wonderful joyous cycle. The more she gave, the happier her heart became. And the more she gave, the more joy she felt in her heart. It was like an infectious deed that everyone around her joined in on.

Amina looked around as the sun dipped below the horizon, the town glowing with the light of her kindness. Her simple actions had stitched together a beautiful weaving of joy and love. Amina's heart swelled with gratitude, for in spreading kindness, she discovered the true meaning of sincerity - doing good for the sake of Allah.

Amina's kindness quest continued in the town where laughter and sunshine never faded, leaving a trail of joy and warmth for everyone to follow.

VALUE 3: HONESTY

AHMED AND THE LOST KITE

A boy named Ahmed lived in a sunny town full of laughter and playful breezes. Ahmed's heart was as bright as the sun, and his eyes sparkled like the clear blue sky. Something colourful caught his eye one day as he strolled through the park with his friends.

A beautiful kite was tangled in the branches of a tall tree. Ahmed's heart skipped a beat as its vibrant colours danced in the wind. As he untangled the kite, a small voice within him said, "Finders, keepers."

But Ahmed was wiser. He knew it was the right thing to do to track down the owner. This was a moral dilemma: keep the fun kite or do what was honest and kind.

Ahmed made a decision based on his firm belief in honesty. He asked around the park, telling everyone he met about the missing kite. His friends, who were drawn in by the colourful discovery, joined him in the search. Ahmed's sincerity created a stir in the park, and soon, children and parents were assisting him in his search for the owner.

After a while, a distraught girl named Layla approached Ahmed. When she saw the familiar kite in his hands, her eyes widened with surprise and joy. "It's my kite!" "I lost it hours ago," she said.

Ahmed smiled warmly, delighted to have located the owner. Layla thanked Ahmed and couldn't stop smiling as she held her kite close to her. The park was alive with excitement as everyone witnessed Ahmed's honesty and Layla's joy.

Ahmed's decision to be truthful benefited the entire community. Parents praised his honesty, and friends admired his sense of being truthful and honest in everything we do.

Ahmed's friends gathered around him as the sun began to set. They discussed how doing the right thing, even when it's difficult, makes everyone feel good. The lost kite became a symbol of Ahmed's honesty, and the story spread throughout town.

Ahmed and his friends were playing in the park the next day, and the air was filled with laughter and the colourful fluttering of kites. Ahmed's decision to return the lost kite sent a ripple of kindness and honesty throughout the community.

So, in a town where the sun always shone and the breeze whispered tales of goodness, Ahmed's story became a reminder that honesty, like a bright kite soaring high, brings joy not just to one person but to the entire community.

VALUE 4: INTEGRITY

Fatima's Fair Play

A girl named Fatima lived in a nice neighbourhood where smiles echoed through the streets. Fatima had a heart as warm as a summer day and a light twinkle in her eye. As she was playing with her friends in the park one day, an idea bloomed in her mind.

"I have an idea, everyone!" Fatima shouted, forming a circle with her friends. "Let's have a special day - a Fair Play Day!"

"What's a Fair Play Day, Fatima?" her friends asked, their eyes shining.

"It's a day where we play games and have fun, but most importantly, we treat everyone with fairness and kindness," Fatima explained with a smile. There will be no cheating or tricks, only fair play!"

As Fatima's friends agreed to the plan, excitement bubbled up like a fizzy soda. They decided to hold races, games, and even share treats to ensure that everyone felt included.

The park was buzzing with excitement as the day of Fair Play arrived. Fatima smiled as she handed out colourful ribbons to each participant. "These ribbons are a reminder to play with integrity," she went on to say.

The first game consisted of a three-legged race. Fatima made sure everyone had a partner and tied soft scarves around their legs. Fatima's friends wobbled and giggled their way to the finish line, filling the air with laughter.

Following on from that was a game of skip-rope and tag. Instead of a single chaser, they played freeze tag, which allowed everyone to run and have fun. Fatima's or sense of fairness, transformed ordinary games into extraordinary moments of joy.

Fatima noticed a few friends sitting alone during a snack break. She invited them to join her group without a second thought, forming a circle of friendship that grew like ripples in a pond.

As the sun began to set, Fatima gathered everyone for one last game: a treasure hunt. Small, glittering treasures were hidden throughout the park, waiting to be discovered. Fatima's friends collaborated, sharing information and discoveries. The joy of discovering treasures was not only in the shiny trinkets, but also in the teamwork and fairness displayed.

Fatima thanked everyone for playing fairly and with kindness, reminding them that treating one another with fairness made the day even more special.

Fatima's Fair Play Day became a treasured memory in a neighbourhood where fairness bloomed like flowers in spring. Her friends carried the lessons of integrity they had learned through games and laughter into their daily lives. Fatima's idea of treating everyone fairly had resulted in a community in which everyone felt valued, included, and, most importantly, treated with fairness.

VALUE 4: INTEGRITY

VALUE 5: GRATITUDE

YOUSSEF'S THANKFUL TREE

A boy named Youssef lived in a vibrant city where the sun painted the sky with warm hues. Youssef had a bright heart and eyes that twinkled with curiosity. One day, as he sat beneath a magnificent oak tree, he reflected on all the wonderful things in his life.

"I have so many blessings in my life, and I want to be grateful for each one," Youssef thought to himself. At that moment, he was inspired to design a Thankful Tree.

Youssef took a handful of brightly coloured paper and cut out leaf shapes. He decided that each leaf would represent something good in his life. With a happy heart, he began to write on each leaf what he was thankful for: family, friends, his pet fish, beautiful weather, and the sense of peace that he felt inside his home.

Youssef's Thankful Tree began to bloom as the days passed. His family noticed the growing tree and decided to join in. Everyone contributed a leaf, sharing their joys and thanks that filled their minds and hearts.

Youssef was faced with a difficult maths problem one day. Frustration set in, but he was reminded of his Thankful Tree. Taking a deep breath, he added a leaf that read "Helpful Teachers," grateful for the assistance that made difficult tasks easier.

Youssef's tree didn't just stay in his house; he took it everywhere with him. His classmates joined in, making their own Thankful Trees. During lunch, they talked about the little things that made them happy, like the smell of fresh cookies or the sound of raindrops on the window.

Youssef's Thankful Tree became a symbol of joy and thanksgiving. It wasn't just about the big things; it was also about appreciating the small pleasures that made each day unique. Youssef found something to be thankful for even on rainy days when the sun was hidden behind clouds - the cosy feeling of a warm blanket or the taste of hot cocoa.

Youssef sat by his Thankful Tree one evening as the sun set and admired its leafy branches. The tree, like his heart, had grown. He realised that expressing gratitude was a journey, a beautiful adventure of appreciating the bounty of blessings all around him.

The Thankful Tree had become a part of Youssef's daily life, a reminder that there was always something to be thankful for, even on the worst of days. It wasn't just saying "thank you"; it was about feeling thankful deep within, cultivating a grateful heart.

So, in a town where gratitude bloomed like flowers in a garden, Youssef's Thankful Tree grew, reminding everyone that a grateful heart makes every day an occasion of happiness and appreciation.

VALUE 6: PATIENCE

LAYLA'S ENCHANTED GARDEN

A little girl named Layla lived in a sunny town where butterflies danced and laughter echoed. Layla had the gentle heart of a whispering breeze and the eyes of morning dew. Layla was inspired by nature's beauty one day and decided to create something special - a fairy-tale garden.

Layla skipped to her backyard, a basket of seeds in one hand and a watering can in the other. She planted tiny seeds with care, envisioning a garden full of colourful flowers and magical moments. She watered her garden every day, hoping to see the first signs of blossoms.

However, as the days passed, Layla saw an issue; the flowers did not bloom as fast as she had hoped. In her heart, she felt a sense of frustration. "Why aren't they growing faster?" she questioned.

Her wise old grandma approached Layla as she sat by her garden one evening. "Patience, little one," she said calmly. "Beautiful things take time to grow."

Layla was moved by those words. She chose beautiful patience, a type of patience that comes from trusting in Allah's perfect timing. Instead of worrying about when the flowers would bloom, Layla concentrated on lovingly tending to her garden.

Layla watered her garden every day, sang to the plants, and even told them stories. Plants, like friendships and dreams, require time to bloom into something beautiful. Layla's patience and care transformed the garden into a magical place, not just because of the colourful flowers.

Layla was tending to her garden one day when she noticed a tiny green sprout peeking through the soil. Her heart was racing wildly. "They're growing!" she screamed, whilst dancing around her garden.

Layla's wonderful garden transformed into an assortment of colours as the weeks passed. Each flower, like a brushstroke on a canvas, painted the garden in red, blue, and yellow hues. Layla's heart warmed as she realised the wait had been worthwhile.

Layla's garden quickly became the talk of the town. Friends and neighbours admired the beauty that had bloomed as a result of Layla's patience. She shared the lessons on patience she had learned, such as how waiting for something nice is similar to waiting for a surprise gift, and how the joy is even greater when it finally arrives.

Layla's captivating garden stood as a reminder that beautiful things, like dreams and friendships, take time to grow. Layla's journey of patience and trust in Allah's timing transformed her garden into a living masterpiece, teaching everyone that the most magical moments come to those who wait patiently and hopeful.

VALUE 7: HUMILITY

OMAR'S HUMBLE PIE

A boy named Omar lived in a cheerful town where soccer balls bounced and goalposts stood tall. Omar had ball-dancing feet and a smile that sparkled like a goal scored at sunset. He was the soccer field's star, known for his incredible skills and quick moves.

Adam approached Omar with a reserved smile one sunny day as he practiced his soccer tricks in the park. "Hey, Omar, can you show me some football skills?" he asked, nervously.

Omar smiled, thrilled with his football skills. "Of course, Adam!" "Watch and learn from the best!" He juggled the ball with his knees, impressing the other kids with his fancy footwork.

Adam's enthusiasm faded as he attempted to imitate Omar's moves, and his football rolled away. Omar was so preoccupied with his own abilities that he didn't notice Adams' struggle. But, as he juggled the ball high in the air, it collided with a branch and fell to the ground.

"Looks like even the best players make mistakes!" Adam chuckled.

Omar felt ashamed as he realised he hadn't paid attention to his friend. "I'm sorry, Adam. "Let me assist you with those moves," he said, his pride giving way to humility.

Omar spent the rest of the day teaching Adam all of his football tricks. He didn't brag; instead, he encouraged and cheered on Adam as he progressed. He even told stories about when he was learning and making mistakes.

Adam's face lit up with a smile as the sun dipped low in the sky. "Thank you so much, Omar!" You're a great teacher."

Omar, the football star, felt a different kind of warmth in his heart. It wasn't the excitement of scoring goals that got me going, but the joy of seeing a friend shine. He realised that true greatness is found not only in personal ability, but also in using that ability to help others.

Omar's attitude shifted from that day forward. He became well-known not only for his outstanding football abilities, but also for his kindness and humility. When he scored a goal, he hugged his teammates and thanked them for their help.

Omar's humility inspired other children to share their talents and help one another grow. The football pitch became a place of encouragement and teamwork, where everyone gave their all and celebrated each other's accomplishments.

As a result, Omar's story of humility became a local legend. The humble spirit transformed the football pitch into a place where everyone could shine, reminding everyone that true greatness is found in lifting others up with a humble and caring heart.

VALUE 7: HUMILITY

VALUE 8: RESPECT FOR PARENTS

AYESHA'S SECRET SURPRISE

Ayesha had a loving heart and a bright smile that brightened the room. One day, as she was thinking about her wonderful parents, an idea struck her - a surprise!

Ayesha made the decision to express her love and gratitude to her parents in a unique way. She moved around the house on tiptoe, planning and whispering to her stuffed animals as if they were her accomplices.

Ayesha crept into the kitchen late at night, when the moon was painting the sky with its gentle glow, to prepare a special breakfast for her parents. She carefully mixed the pancake batter, making sure not to make any noise. The aroma of pancakes filled the air, and Ayesha couldn't help but smile as she thought about her secret mission.

She then collected colourful paper and markers to make handmade cards. Each card expressed her love and gratitude for her mother and father. Ayesha poured her heart into every marker stroke, creating a work of art that spoke louder than words.

Ayesha set the dining table with the delicately made pancakes and placed the handmade cards next to each plate. She crept into her parents' room, gently waking them up with a "Surprise!"

Her parents followed Ayesha to the dining table, still half-asleep. They were overjoyed when they saw the special breakfast and heartfelt cards. Ayesha smiled, pleased to see her surprise working like a charm.

"Wow! What a delightful surprise. Thank you!" her mother declared, her eyes welling up with tears of joy.

"This is the best breakfast ever," Ayesha's father added. You certainly know how to make our day memorable."

Ayesha's parents felt a warm glow in their hearts all morning. They realised that Ayesha's secret surprise was more than just pancakes and cards; it was a beautiful display of love and respect.

Ayesha's parents discovered more surprises as the day progressed. A tidy room, freshly picked flowers in a vase, and small notes of thanks hidden around the house. Ayesha's actions revealed her admiration and love for her parents.

That evening, as they sat on the living room floor, Ayesha expressed her emotions. "I just wanted to say how much I appreciate and enjoy everything you do for me." You are the most wonderful parents on the planet."

Her parents hugged Ayesha tightly, filled with joy and gratitude. Ayesha's surprise had created a bond of love and respect in their home, making it even warmer and pleasant.

As a result, Ayesha's secret surprise became a treasured memory in the cosy little house where love flowed like a gentle stream. The story of respect for parents echoed through the walls, reminding everyone that simple acts of love and gratitude can bring a family world of happiness.

VALUE 9: KINDNESS

KHALID'S KINDNESS CREW

A boy named Khalid lived in a lively little neighbourhood. Khalid had a soft heart and a smile that could brighten even the darkest of days. One day, while playing with his friends, he had an idea that would transform their community - the "Kindness Crew."

Khalid gathered his friends and told them about his plan. "Let's form a Kindness Crew to spread kindness all over our neighbourhood. We can help those in need while also improving the area we live in!" We can help those in need while also making our community even better!"

As Khalid's friends joined the Kindness Crew, excitement grew. They talked about various acts of kindness and decided to begin with something simple but meaningful.

Their first mission was to assemble "Kindness Kits" filled with snacks, water, and encouraging notes. The Kindness Crew went around the neighbourhood, delivering these surprise packages to elderly neighbours, homeless people and families in need. The smiles they received in return were like sunshine shining through the clouds.

The crew, motivated by their success, took on bigger challenges. They planned a neighbourhood clean-up day, picking up litter and sprucing up the streets. Sara, a friend of Khalid's, said, "It feels good to make our home beautiful for everyone."

Khalid learned about a new family in the neighbourhood who had recently relocated from afar one day. The Kindness Crew greeted them warmly, bringing them homemade cookies and showing them around. From the first day, the new family felt like they belonged.

The generosity spread like a ripple, touching every corner of the community. The Kindness Crew assisted children with their homework, planted flowers in the community garden, and even planned a "Share and Care" day in which everyone brought something to share with others.

Khalid and his friends began to notice something amazing happening as the days passed. The neighbourhood became a place where people looked out for one another, where there were lots of smiles and greetings, and where everyone felt like they were part of a big, caring family.

The Kindness Crew not only spread kindness, but also built a supportive and loving community. Khalid realised that kindness had the power to change the world, beginning in their own backyard.

Khalid's Kindness Crew became a beacon of kindness in the lively neighbourhood. Their acts of kindness became legendary, inspiring children to believe in the power of kindness wherever they went.

VALUE 10: GENEROSITY

NADIA'S SHARING PICNIC

Nadia was a cheerful girl living in a happy town full of butterflies and giggles. Nadia had a heart as warm as a summer day. She had a brilliant idea one day while sitting in her garden.

Nadia invited all of her friends, neighbours to the picnic to share snacks. The only requirement was that everyone bring a tasty treat.

Nadia's friends arrived on the picnic day, each with a basket full of their favourite treats. Cookies, sandwiches, fruits, and even homemade lemonade were available.

Nadia initiated the sharing circle with a generous heart. "Let's pass the snacks around the table. We'll have a little bit of everything this way, and everyone will be able to enjoy it!" she said.

Ali was the first to share, having brought his grandmother's famous chocolate chip cookies. As everyone reached for a cookie, the sweet aroma filled the air.

Sara brought some refreshing watermelon slices, and the picnic quickly became a colourful feast. The joy of generosity was spreading, and strangers felt like old friends, united by the simple act of sharing.

Mr. Patel, the friendly neighbour across the street, joined in on the fun with his spicy samosas. The kids were wide-eyed and excited as they tasted flavours they hadn't tried before. Nadia's Sharing Picnic evolved into a melting pot of flavours and cultures.

Something special happened as the picnic progressed. Nadia noticed that the picnic blankets were no longer divided into groups. Instead, everyone sat together, sharing snacks, stories, and laughter as if they'd known each other forever.

Nadia's heart swelled with joy as she looked around at the happy faces. It was more than just a picnic; it was a celebration of generosity and community.

Nadia's mother, couldn't be more proud of her daughter. "You've made something lovely, Nadia. You've demonstrated to everyone that generosity brings people together and strengthens the community we live in."

The sharing circle stood for a group photo as the evening came in. The picnic had become a memory, a treasured moment of generosity and unity.

Nadia's Sharing Picnic became a tradition. The story of her generous spirit inspired others to embrace the joy of sharing, and giving in the neighbourhood and making everyone feel like family.

VALUE 10: GENEROSITY

VALUE 11: FORGIVENESS

ELIAS AND THE FRIENDSHIP FORGIVENESS

Elias and Amir were best friends in a neighbourhood where laughter filled the air, making every day a fantastic adventure of fun. They were inseparable, laughing and going on adventures together like two peas in a pod.

In Elias' backyard, Elias and Amir were constructing a cardboard box fort. A disagreement arose as they planned and crafted. It started with a disagreement about how the fort should be built and turned into hurtful words.

Amir decided to abandon the fort-building adventure because he was upset. With an uneasy feeling in his stomach, Elias watched his friend walk away. The sunny day had turned cloudy and depressing.

Days turned into weeks, and Elias and Amir's friendship remained strained. They passed each other without a smile or a wave, and the joy of their shared adventures faded into the distance that separated them.

Elias sat on his porch one evening, staring at the unfinished fort in the backyard. He yearned for the laughter and the friendship, with his friend Amir.

Elias decided to take the first step towards repairing their friendship. He went to Amir's house with a peace offering: a drawing of their fort that combined both of their ideas. Amir opened the door, surprised and intrigued, to find Elias holding the drawing.

"I apologise for what happened, Amir. I miss our laughs and adventures. Can we finish the fort together?" Elias asked, his eyes reflecting the seriousness of his words.

Amir looked at the drawing before turning to face Elias. A brief moment of silence followed, followed by a small smile on Amir's lips. "I miss our adventures as well, Elias." Let's work together to finish the fort."

Elias and Amir put aside their differences and focused on the joy of construction, creation, and, most importantly, forgiveness. The laughter returned as they worked side by side, echoing through the backyard.

Elias and Amir realised that disagreements happen, but it is the ability to forgive and move on that strengthens friendships.

As the sun set over the finished fort, Elias and Amir sat inside, sharing stories and snacks. The power of forgiveness had not only rebuilt their fort but also strengthened their friendship.

As a result, Elias and Amir's Friendship Forgiveness became a story of resilience and understanding. The story of their fort served as a reminder that forgiveness is a powerful tool capable of mending even the strongest bonds, transforming cloudy days into sunny adventures once more.

VALUE 12: GOOD MANNERS

SARA'S SWEET WORDS

A girl named Sara lived in a pleasant town where the sun painted the skies with warm tones. Sara had a sunflower-colored heart and a smile that sparkled like morning dew. She discovered something incredible one day while playing with her friends and talking with her family.

Sara's adventure began when her younger brother, Ali, knocked over her tower of building blocks by accident. Rather than becoming upset, Sara took a deep breath and said, "It's all right, Ali. Accidents occur. Let's rebuild it together!"

Her kind words had a magical effect. Ali's face lit up with a smile as they worked together to build an even bigger and better tower. Sara discovered that saying "It's okay" and using polite language made everything feel better.

"Thank you, Ahmad!" Sara stated this after Ahmad had shared his snacks with her. "That's very thoughtful of you." The words of gratitude made Ahmad happy, and he smiled, knowing that his generosity had been noticed.

Sara's mother served her favourite spaghetti for dinner that night. Instead of digging in, Sara asked her mother, "Please may I have some more spaghetti?" Sara's mother, who was pleased with her daughter's demeanour, gladly served her an extra helping.

The magic words and politeness did not end there. After a long day at work, Sara's father was fixing a broken toy for Ali. "Dad, can I help you with that?" Sara said. Her father smiled proudly, grateful for Sara's thoughtful offer.

Something amazing happened as Sara continued to sprinkle her conversations with "please," "thank you," and "excuse me." Her friends and family began to use these beautiful words as well. The house was filled with the harmony of good manners, and the air felt lighter.

Sara's teacher noticed the positive change in the classroom one day. Students were saying "excuse me" when they needed to pass and "thank you" when they were helped. "Class," Sara's teacher said with a twinkle in her eye, "I see a lot of kind words and good manners here." Continue your excellent work!"

Sara, now aware of the power she had wielded, continued to spread kindness with her words. "I'm here for you," Sara said to her friend Amirah when she was sad. "You're not by yourself." Sarah's frown soon turned into a smile as the power of empathy and good manners worked wonders.

Sara's Sweet Words became a legend in the cosy town where the sun painted the skies with warm hues. The news of her discovery spread quickly, inspiring both children and adults to believe in the power of good manners. The town blossomed with respectful conversations and harmonious relationships, proving that the most enchanting magic can be created with the simplest words.

VALUE 13: DIGNITY

ZAINAB'S STAND FOR JUSTICE

Once upon a time, a girl named Zainab lived in a small village by the countryside where the flowers blossomed. Zainab had a heart as big as a mountain and a spirit that radiated kindness. One day, she witnessed something that sparked a fire within her.

Aisha, a quiet and thoughtful girl, was frequently the target of cruel remarks from a group of students at school. Zainab, sensing the injustice, couldn't stand by and watch her friend feel hurt. She decided it was time to speak up.

Zainab approached Aisha as the school bell rang, signalling the end of the day. "I've noticed how those kids treat you, Aisha, and it's not right. Let's talk to our teacher about it and figure out how to make it stop."

Aisha nodded, moved by Zainab's bravery. The two friends went to their teacher's class, ready to tell all. Zainab described the situation, her words ringing with determination to find a solution to this problem.

Mrs. Johnson, their teacher, listened intently and admired Zainab's bravery in standing up for her friend. She decided to address the problem in front of the entire class, emphasising the importance of treating one another with kindness and respect.

Mrs. Johnson spoke to the students the next day in class about the importance of dignity, and how everyone has the right to be treated fairly. Aisha began to feel a sense of respect and fairness she had not previously felt.

Zainab's efforts did not end there. She organised a "Dignity Day" at her school, during which students made posters and shared stories about the importance of treating others with kindness and dignity. Messages of respect and understanding echoed off the school's walls.

Aisha's once-unfair treatment became a triumphant story. Zainab's stand for justice not only changed the atmosphere in the classroom, but it also sparked a kindness and dignity movement throughout the school.

Zainab's bravery became an inspiration to other children who had faced injustice. They, too, began to speak up for what was right, fostering a culture of respect. The village was transformed into a place where every child felt valued and dignified.

As a result, Zainab's Stand for Justice became a story of bravery and compassion. The story inspired children to embrace preserving their own dignity and standing up to injustice, transforming their town into a haven of kindness and respect.

VALUE 14: LOYALTY

AMIN AND THE FRIENDSHIP TREE

One day, a girl named Hiba, who lived in a jolly little neighbourhood, was strolling through the park one day, she came across a Friendship Tree.

The tree was tall and sturdy, with branches that reached out like welcoming arms. Hiba noticed colourful ribbons tied to the tree's branches, each with a memory shared by friends. Hiba's eyes widened with curiosity as she approached the tree, wondering about its history.

A wise old neighbor, Mrs. Ann, approached Hiba with a twinkle in her eye. "Ah, Hiba, this is the Friendship Tree. Every ribbon represents a special memory and the enduring strength of true friendship."

Hiba was intrigued and decided to make her own ribbon for the Friendship Tree. She gathered his friends - Zara, Jameila, and Leila - and set out on adventures to create memories to last a lifetime.

Their first ribbon was bright red, representing the day they had a sleepover in Hiba's house. They had a few chuckles, ate biscuits, and shared funny secrets. Hiba tied the ribbon to a low-hanging branch, and the Friendship Tree got a new memory.

Hiba and her friends continued to add ribbons to the tree as the days turned into weeks. Each ribbon told a story: when they rescued a trapped kitten, when they planted flowers in the neighbourhood garden, and when they laughed until their stomachs hurt.

Hiba was faced with a challenge one day. Her family was relocating to a new town, and she was concerned about leaving behind the Friendship Tree and her friends. Mrs. Ann smiled as she handed Amin a special ribbon - a golden one. "This ribbon symbolises loyalty and the enduring bond of true friends. Tie it to the tree, Hiba, and know that your bond will endure wherever you go."

Hiba tied the golden ribbon to a sturdy branch with a mix of joy and sadness. She whispered visits and letters, knowing that true friendship, like the golden ribbon, could endure any distance.

Years passed, and Hiba returned to town. The Friendship Tree, now adorned with various coloured ribbons, stood as a testament to the enduring strength of loyalty. Hiba, Zara, Jameila, and Leila gathered around the tree, recalling the memories they had made.

The golden ribbon sparkled in the sunlight, untouched by time. Hiba realised that the golden ribbon represented loyalty, which was at the heart of their friendship. The Friendship Tree stood as an ongoing tribute to the value of loyalty and commitment that binds friends together through thick and thin, regardless of the miles, years, or changes.

The story celebrated the enduring strength of true friendship, teaching children the importance of loyalty and the beauty of making their own Friendship Tree.

VALUE 15: RESPECT FOR ELDERS

GRANDMA'S TEA PARTY

Once upon a time, there was a young boy named Rashid who was eager to learn and discover new things. Rashid grew up with a wise grandmother who had a heart full of stories and eyes that sparkled with wisdom. They decided to throw a special tea party one sunny afternoon.

Rashid kept his eyes wide open as Grandma carefully prepared a cup of tea. The tea leaves swirled in the pot, releasing scents that seemed to hold the secrets of a hundred stories. Recognising the Rashid's interest, Grandma smiled and said, "Today, we're not just having tea; we're having a Wisdom Tea Party."

The teacups and saucers twinkled in the sunlight as they sat at the small table. Grandma poured the tea and began telling stories about her adventures, times when she faced difficulties and triumphs. Rashid sat quietly, taking in the wisdom that flowed like a gentle stream.

Grandma's first lesson in patience. "Patience is a virtue, my dear, just like tea takes time to brew. "Those who wait will be rewarded." Rashid nodded, understanding that some things, like tea, take time to develop into something extraordinary.

Grandma spoke about kindness as they sipped their tea. "Kindness is like adding sugar to tea, sweetheart." It improves everything. Be kind to others, and you'll notice how your world improves." The child smiled, imagining a world full of kindness like a perfectly sweetened cup of tea.

The following lesson was about gratitude. "Every sip of tea is a reason to be thankful." Every day is a gift, just like that. Be thankful for the small pleasures, and your heart will be as warm as a cup of tea on a cold winter day." Rashid embraced the concept with warmth and appreciation.

Grandma's stories continued, addressing issues such as honesty, resilience, and love. Rashid's heart swelled with admiration for Grandma's wisdom as each lesson was a sip from the cup of life.

"Remember, my dear, there's a world of wisdom in respecting and learning from your elders," Grandma said as the Wisdom Tea Party came to an end. We carry stories, lessons, and love to help you navigate life."

Rashid hugged Grandma tightly, grateful for the valuable lessons they had learned during their special tea party. Rashid not only respected Grandma's wisdom after that, but he also realised the value of seeking advice from elders.

Grandma's Wisdom Tea Party became a cherished memory of respecting and learning from elders who carry the sweet wisdom of life in the cosy little house where the aroma of cookies danced in the air.

VALUE 16: RESPONSIBILITY

Hana's Responsible Rabbit

A girl named Hana lived in a neighbourhood filled with children's laughter and the rustling of leaves. Hana had a gentle heart and a spirit that yearned for adventure. She discovered a little bunny rabbit with soft fur and floppy ears hopping around near her garden one sunny day.

Hana's eyes twinkled with delight. She gave the rabbit the name Milo and decided to keep her as a pet. Hana knew she had to care for Milo with love and dedication.

Hana's first task was to make Milo a comfortable home. She discovered an old basket, lined it with soft blankets, and placed it in a peaceful corner of her room. Milo hopped into her new home, her nose wagging in approval.

The following item on the agenda was feeding time. Hana researched rabbit food and made sure Milo had a variety of fresh vegetables and hay. Her small ears twitched with delight as Milo nibbled on a carrot.

Hana and Milo developed a special bond as the days turned into weeks. Milo hopped alongside Hana as they explored the wonders of nature on their garden adventures. Hana was filled with joy and purpose as she realised she was fulfilling her responsibility by taking good care of her furry friend.

Hana noticed Milo looking lonely one evening as the sun painted the sky with orange and pink hues. She made the thoughtful decision to introduce Milo to the other rabbits in the neighbourhood. Milo soon had new friends to hop and play with after she organised a Bunny Playdate.

Hana's sense of duty extended beyond simply feeding and sheltering Milo. She accepted responsibility for Milo's happiness and social life, understanding that being a good pet owner entailed more than just the basics.

When a friend invited Hana to a party, she hesitated, remembering Milo. Recognising her responsibilities, she sought advice from her mother. Hana's friend was overjoyed when she brought Milo to the party, and everyone had a good time with the fluffy visitor.

Hana's sense of responsibility towards Milo became second nature as the days passed. She found satisfaction in carrying out her responsibilities, and Milo, with her soft fur and twitching nose, became a symbol of responsibility and love in Hana's life.

As a result, this became a story of commitment and care in a neighbourhood filled with children's laughter and the rustling of leaves. The story of Hana and Milo helped children understand that teaching them that responsibilities, no matter how big or small, give our lives meaning and fulfilment.

VALUE 16: RESPONSIBILITY

VALUE 17: CLEANLINESS

ADAM'S CLEAN-UP ADVENTURE

One sunny day, while playing with his friends in the park, Adam noticed something that made him sad: litter was scattered everywhere and made the park unsafe and not nice. This made Adam feel very sad.

Adam had a burning desire to want to change this so he decided it was time for a Clean-up Adventure. He gathered his friends - Yahya, Omar, and Layla - and set out to make their town sparkle, armed with gloves, trash bags, and a positive attitude.

The park was their first stop, where colourful wrappers danced in the wind like mischievous butterflies. "Let's turn this into a Clean-up Adventure!" Adam yelled, with an enthusiastic shimmer in his eyes. "The person who collects the most trash will receive a special surprise."

Excitedly, Adam's friends rushed around, picking up wrappers, bottles, and stray papers. They talked and laughed, making the clean-up a game. Layla found a rejected soccer ball, while Yahya found an abandoned teddy bear. The park had been transformed into a thrilling treasure hunt.

Adam noticed something magical happening as they gathered the last of the litter. The once-clogged park was now spotless, and the friends felt a sense of accomplishment. The trees seemed to sway in thanks, and the flowers bloomed brighter, as if applauding the Clean-up Adventure team's efforts.

But Adam's concern didn't end there. He realised that, just like the environment, our hearts needed to be cleaned. The friends decided to embark on a spiritual Clean-up Adventure after being inspired by their success. They gathered at Adam's house, where his mother instilled in them the value of cleanliness in both the physical and spiritual realms.

The friends discovered how to cleanse their intentions, thoughts, and actions. They discovered the beauty of ablution before prayer, a form of spiritual cleanliness that brought them peace. The friends felt a sense of connection and serenity as they prayed together, realising the importance of cleanliness in their lives.

Adam's Clean-up Adventure spread throughout the town, inspiring other children to participate. The bustling town was transformed into a haven of cleanliness, with children picking up litter and learning the value of spiritual purity.

Adam's Clean-up Adventure became a legend in the vibrant town where the sun kissed the flowers and the air was filled with laughter. The story has been passed down through the generations, teaching children about the benefits of cleanliness on the environment and personal well-being. The town glistened not only from the sun's rays, but also from the collective effort of its residents to keep it clean - a shining example of the values of cleanliness and purity.

VALUE 18: CONTENTMENT

KAMRAN'S SIMPLE TREASURES

A young boy named Kamran lived in a bustling city where the streets were alive with activity. His family lived in a modest flat, and while their belongings were modest, their home exuded warmth and love. Kamran, on the other hand, was constantly envious of his friends' new toys and gadgets.

Kamran decided to investigate the value of contentment with what he already had after overhearing his parents discuss their financial situation one day. He set out on a mission to find joy in the normal aspects of his daily life.

Kamran began by organising a family game night, during which laughter could be heard echoing throughout their cosy apartment. Kamran realised that the joy of spending time together outweighed the fleeting excitement of new toys as they played board games and shared stories.

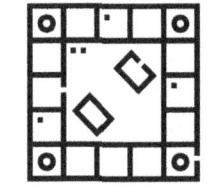

He then discovered a small garden patch on their balcony, which his mother meticulously maintained. Kamran was inspired and joined her in planting vibrant flowers and herbs. The simple act of caring for the plants gave them a sense of accomplishment and appreciation for the beauty in their surroundings.

Kamran was sitting on the balcony one evening when he noticed the sky transforming into a canvas of hues during sunset. He took out a sketchpad and began to capture the beauty of the moment. Another treasure in his life was the simple joy of expressing himself through art.

Kamran and his family decided to declutter their home over the weekend. Kamran discovered forgotten toys and books while sorting through their belongings, which caught his interest. These rediscovered possessions became a source of delight, demonstrating that contentment is frequently found in appreciating what one already has.

Kamran's path to happiness extended beyond his home. He volunteered at a local community centre, realising that helping others bring a different kind of richness to his life.

Kamran discovered a profound sense of contentment as he embraced the simplicity of his possessions and focused on the meaningful experiences around him. His family, once concerned about not being able to provide the most up-to-date toys, discovered joy in shared moments and simple treasures that enriched their lives.

As a result, in a city where desires frequently overshadow contentment, Kamran's story became a reminder that true wealth is found in appreciating the simple, often overlooked treasures that surround us every day.

VALUE 19: COURAGE

KARIM'S BRAVE QUEST

Karim, a lively boy, lived in a lively neighbourhood where the sound of children playing filled the air. While Karim enjoyed exploring his surroundings, he was often frightened when faced with new challenges. Karim hesitated, unsure if he had the courage to join his friends as they climbed the tallest trees or slid down the steepest slides.

Karim overheard his parents discussing an upcoming talent show in their neighbourhood one day. Karim's heart raced with excitement as he imagined himself on stage sharing his passion for storytelling. However, the prospect of performing in front of a crowd made him nervous and uncertain.

Karim decided to embark on a courageous journey in order to overcome his fears. He started by asking his friends about their own encounters with fear and bravery. Their stories moved him, teaching him that courage was not the absence of fear, but the strength to face it.

He spent weeks crafting a thrilling story about a daring young adventurer, drawing inspiration from his own experiences. Nerves pulled at Karim as the show date approached, but he persisted, determined to tell his story.

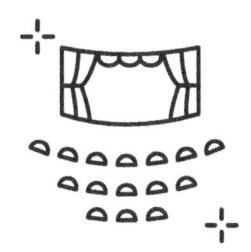

Karim took a deep breath and stepped onto the stage on the night of the talent show. The spotlight shone on him, and the hushed audience felt like a vast forest waiting to hear his story. Karim's voice grew stronger with each word as he began to speak, and the audience was captivated by his bravery and storytelling prowess.

Karim's bravery not only earned him the community's admiration, but it also ignited a spark within him. He realised that courage was more than just facing physical challenges; it was also about seizing opportunities to share his unique voice and talents.

Karim continued to take brave steps after that, whether it was standing up for a friend, trying new activities, or pursuing his passions. His journey taught the neighbourhood that courage was the triumph over fear rather than the absence of fear—a valuable lesson that inspired those around him to face their fears with determination and bravery.

Karim's story became a testament to the positive power of courage and the incredible heights one could reach by taking bold and courageous steps in the lively neighbourhood where children played and dreams took flight.

VALUE 19: COURAGE

VALUE 20: OPTIMISM

FARAH'S DAY OF HAPPINESS

Farah lived in a town where the clouds danced with the sun and raindrops painted pictures on the pavement. Farah had a feather-light heart and eyes that sparkled with curiosity. Aisha decided to be optimistic one gloomy day as rain tapped on her window.

Farah put on her brightest raincoat and gathered her friends, Ali and Fatima, with a positive attitude. Although the sky was grey, Farah saw the promise of colour hidden in the clouds. "Even if the sun is hiding, let's find our own rainbow!"

Their laughter echoed in the rain as the friends skipped through puddles. "Look!" said Farah, pointing to the sky. Each raindrop is a tiny painter, and they work together to create the most beautiful art." Inspired by Farah's optimism, Ali and Fatima began to see the beauty in the rain.

Farah noticed a garden where flowers bloomed despite the rain as they walked through town. "Isn't it wonderful how the flowers soak up the rain and continue to smile even when the sun is hiding?" she blurted out. Ali and Fatima, who were both wearing bright colours - Ali with a bright umbrella and Fatima with vibrant boots - agreed that there was beauty in every drop.

Their next stop was the park, where they discovered a large enough puddle for splashing. "Let us make a wish on every splash and see if Allah will grant our wishes!" Farah said, her eyes twinkling. Ali wished for a massive chocolate cake, while Fatima wished for a day filled with endless laughter. Farah wished for more joyful rainy days. The friends laughed as they realised that even wishes in the rain could bring smiles.

A brief ray of sunlight shone through as the clouds separated. "Look!" yelled Farah. "The sun is sending us a message in code." She pointed to the sky, where a faint rainbow appeared, its colours stretching like a bridge of hope across the horizon. The friends twirled and danced as if they had discovered a pot of rainbow gold.

"Today we found beauty in the rain, joy in the puddles, and even a rainbow at the end," Farah said as they drove home, drenched but full of the warmth of friendship and optimism. Imagine how every grey day can be turned into a happy day if we choose to look on the bright side!"

As a result, the story spread throughout town like sunshine after rain, reminding children that they can find hope and happiness even in the most difficult circumstances. Farah's optimistic spirit left a rainbow in the hearts of all who heard her colourful story.

VALUE 21: MODESTY

Jamal's Modesty Show

A boy named Jamal lived in a town where the wind whispered stories of kindness and the flowers bloomed with humility. Jamal's heart was as gentle as a breeze, and his smile radiated warmth. Jamal decided to organise a Modesty Show one day after being inspired by the idea of showcasing the beauty of modesty.

Jamal gathered his friends - Tayab, Ahmed, and Amina - with excitement in his heart. They agreed that the fashion show would be about embracing modesty in their choices rather than the flashiest clothes or the brightest colours.

Each friend brought clothes that reflected their individual style while adhering to Hayaa's modesty values. Amina wore a beautiful scarf that sparkled with humility, while Tayab wore a simple buttoned shirt with sleeves. Jamal wore a plain, elegant suit, while Ahmed chose a comfortable outfit that covered him modestly.

They realised as they walked down the park's "modesty runway" that dressing with Hayaa was more than just clothing; it was a reflection of their personality. The audience, which included friends and family members, applauded not only for the fashion but also for the values it represented.

To make the show even more special, each friend shared their definition of modesty. Tayab discussed the beauty of feeling at ease and confident in simple clothing. Amina emphasised the grace and dignity that came with wearing a head covering. Ahmed explained that modesty goes beyond clothing and includes how we speak and carry ourselves. Jamal discussed the value of humility and kindness in all aspects of life.

The Modesty Show was more than just a fashion show; it became a celebration of the values that adorned the participants' hearts. The friends realised that modesty was liberating, allowing them to express their individuality while upholding their values.

The friends decided to make the Modesty Show a regular event as the sun set below the horizon, casting a warm glow on the modest runway. They hoped to inspire others to embrace modesty in their choices and behaviours, recognising the beauty of humility.

Jamal's Modesty Show quickly spread throughout the town, and other children soon joined in. The park was transformed into a runway of diversity, with children proudly displaying their individual styles while adhering to modesty principles.

Jamal's Modesty Show became a cherished tradition in the town where the wind whispered tales of kindness and the flowers bloomed with humility. The story was passed down through the generations, encouraging children to embrace modesty not only in their clothing but also in their actions and choices, resulting in a town where humility was the fashion that never went out of style.

VALUE 22: TRUTHFULNESS

Zara's Truth Telling Adventure

Zara lived in a town where the trees whispered stories of integrity. Zara had a pure heart as clear as a crystal stream and a curious spirit. She found herself on a Truth Telling Adventure one day while playing in the park with her friends.

Zara's adventure started when she discovered a magical map that promised exciting discoveries if she told the truth. Zara, intrigued, gathered her friends Samir, Aisha, and Omar. They unfolded the map together, revealing a path that led to the heart of the Enchanted Forest.

They encountered talking animals and friendly fairies as they travelled through the forest. The map, however, stated that if anyone told a lie, the path would vanish. Zara assured her friends, "No matter what, let's always tell the truth!"

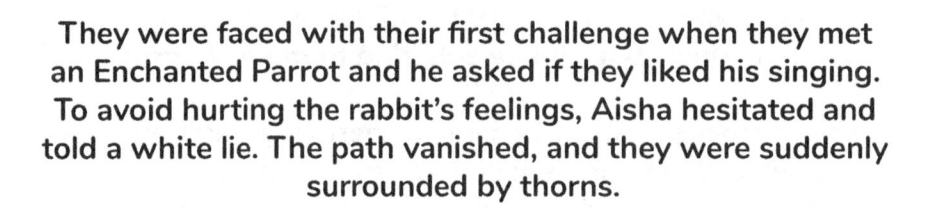

They were faced with their first challenge when they met an Enchanted Parrot and he asked if they liked his singing. To avoid hurting the rabbit's feelings, Aisha hesitated and told a white lie. The path vanished, and they were suddenly surrounded by thorns.

Aisha quickly admitted her mistake after realising the consequences of dishonesty. The magical map, sensing her sincerity, revealed the path once more. The friends continued their adventure with renewed zeal, having realised the value of truth.

As they approached the Talking Tree, it posed a difficult riddle. Omar, who is known for his wit, considered pretending to know the answer. Zara, remembering the Enchanted Rabbit's lesson, encouraged him to be truthful before he could speak. Despite his embarrassment, Omar admitted he didn't know the answer. Surprisingly, the Talking Tree, pleased with their candour, led them to the next section of the forest.

The adventure took them through colourful flower meadows and sparkling water streams. The friends chose truth over deception in each challenge, and the magical map rewarded them with beautiful sights and newfound friendships.

Finally, they arrived at the Enchanted Forest's Heart, where the Wise Owl awaited. The owl praised them for their honesty and revealed the greatest reward of all: a treasure chest filled with the joy of knowing they had acted with integrity, rather than gold.

When Zara and her friends returned from their Truth Telling Adventure, they realised that honesty was more than just a magical map requirement; it was a treasure that strengthened their bonds and made their journey more meaningful. The Enchanted Forest came to represent the positive effects of honesty on relationships and personal integrity.

Zara's Truth Telling Adventure became a legend in the town where the sun painted rainbows in the sky and the trees whispered tales of honesty. The story echoed in children's hearts, teaching them that the path of truthfulness leads to the most enchanting adventures and the most precious treasures of all.

VALUE 23: SELF-DISCIPLINE

RAYAN'S SELF-DISCIPLINE SUPERPOWER

Rayan had a heart as steady as a compass needle and determination in his eyes. One day, while contemplating how to make his dreams a reality, he discovered a hidden superpower - the power of self-discipline.

Rayan's superpower had nothing to do with flying or wearing a cape. It was the ability to control his desires and precisely manage his actions. Rayan, ecstatic about his newfound strength, decided to use his superpower to face challenges and make his dreams a reality.

Rayan's first challenge was to complete his homework before playing his favourite video game. The allure of the game tempted him like a mischievous sprite as he sat at his desk. Rayan, on the other hand, remained focused on his homework and completed it flawlessly.

His superpowers did not end there. Rayan realised he could use it to eat healthy snacks rather than sugary treats. He chose fruits and nuts over candies because he wanted to stay strong and healthy, and he felt a boost of energy from his disciplined choices.

Rayan's superpower quickly spread throughout the neighbourhood, and other children sought his advice. Aleena, tempted by the call of the television, inquired about Rayan's ability to complete his chores before screen time. Rayan revealed the secret to self-discipline: setting priorities and sticking to them tenaciously.

Rayan decided to organise a superhero-themed event in his neighbourhood, inspired by the positive impact of his self-discipline superpower. Children dressed up as their favourite superheroes, and Rayan, dressed in a homemade superhero costume, took on the role of Captain Self-discipline.

Captain Self-discipline led a series of self-discipline challenges during the event. The children discovered the strength within themselves to control their actions, from balancing on one foot to resisting the temptation of a delicious but unnecessary snack.

Rayan felt a sense of accomplishment as the event came to a close. His superpower of self-discipline had not only aided him, but had also inspired others to embrace this important life skill.

Rayan's journey continued, and with each new challenge, his superpower of self-discipline grew stronger. Whether it was doing chores, practicing healthy habits, or focusing on his studies, Rayan understood that self-discipline was a lifelong skill that allowed him to shape his own destiny.

Rayan's Self-discipline Superpower became a story of empowerment and determination. The story resonated in children's hearts, teaching them that the ability to control desires and manage actions was a superhero strength within each of them, waiting to be discovered and unleashed.

VALUE 24: ENVIRONMENTAL PROTECTION

SADIA AND THE GREEN TEAM

Sadia had the gentle heart of a morning dewdrop and the eyes of a nature lover. Sadia had an idea that would blossom into a wonderful adventure one sunny day as she explored the park with her friends - forming the Green Team.

Sadia gathered her friends - Ahmed, Aisha, and Omar - with glee. They put on matching green hats and took on the role of environmental defenders. Sadia went on to say, "We are the Green Team, and our mission is to take care of our planet, just like superheroes for Earth!"

The Green Team's first assignment was to clean up the park. They scurried around like busy bees, armed with gloves and trash bags, picking up litter and cleaning up the playground. "Every piece of trash we pick up is a gift to the Earth," Sadia explained with a twinkle in her eye. It's like a big green hug for our planet!"

The Green Team discovered the magic of recycling while working. Sadia taught her friends how to sort their trash into plastic, paper, and glass, turning their cleanup into a recycling adventure. Aisha was giggling as she said, "It's like giving these materials a second chance at a happy life!"

Inspired by their success, the Green Team decided to share their enthusiasm for nature with the entire town. They organised a tree-planting day in which families came together to plant saplings in the park. "These trees will grow big and strong, just like our love for the environment," Sadia said, holding a tiny tree in her hands. It is our way of saying 'thank you' to Allah!"

The efforts of the Green Team did not end there. They started a community garden where neighbours could grow fruits and vegetables together. Sadia, proudly wearing her green hat, explained, "Growing our food is like having a picnic with the Earth." We're looking after it, and it's looking after us!"

As word of the Green Team's exploits spread, more children joined their cause. Families composted, used reusable bags, and took shorter showers to save water, transforming the town into a canvas of green initiatives. Sadia's idea had grown into a town-wide environmental stewardship movement.

The Green Team celebrated the positive impact of their actions as the seasons changed. The park was blooming with vibrant flowers, the air was cleaner, and the once-diminished trees stood tall and proud. Sadia, surrounded by her green-hatted friends, beams with pride.

Sadia and the Green Team became legends in the town where the flowers whispered secrets to the trees and the breeze carried tales of responsibility. The story resonated in the hearts of children, inspiring them to become environmental stewards, realising that small actions can make a big difference in caring for the world around them.

VALUE 25: FRIENDSHIP

TAHIR'S UNBREAKABLE BOND

Tahir, a cheerful boy, lived in a close-knit neighbourhood where laughter echoed through the streets. Tahir treasured his friendships, understanding the profound importance of friendship in his life. He had no idea that a one-of-a-kind adventure would strengthen these bonds and teach him the true meaning of companionship.

The neighbourhood decided to start a community garden one summer day. Families came together to plant flowers, herbs, and vegetables, transforming a barren lot into a vibrant space bursting with the colours of unity and collaboration. Tahir was ecstatic to take part and invited his closest friends to join him in the gardening venture.

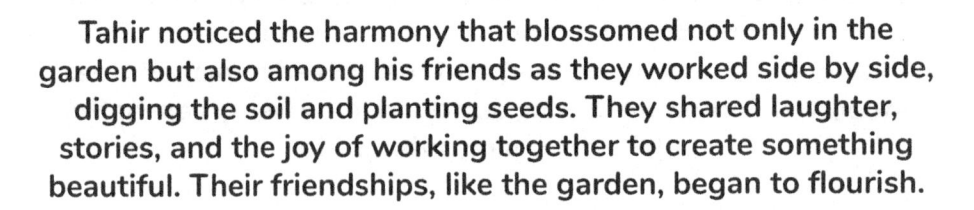

Tahir noticed the harmony that blossomed not only in the garden but also among his friends as they worked side by side, digging the soil and planting seeds. They shared laughter, stories, and the joy of working together to create something beautiful. Their friendships, like the garden, began to flourish.

A sudden storm, however, threatened to wash away their hard work. Tahir and his friends rushed to protect the vulnerable plants, realising that the storm represented the difficulties that life could bring. Tahir realised at that moment the profound Islamic value of friendship—supporting one another through life's storms.

Tahir and his friends huddled together, shielding the garden with their bodies as the rain fell and the wind howled. Their bond was unbreakable, much like the unwavering support that true friends offer in times of adversity. The storm passed, leaving nothing but a garden that had withstood the test, much like their friendships.

Tahir and his friends were inspired by this experience and decided to share the garden's harvest with the community. They planned a neighbourhood feast and invited everyone to enjoy the fruits of their collective labour. Giving strengthened the community's sense of unity, transforming the community garden into a symbol of friendship's enduring power.

Through this adventure, Tahir discovered that true friendship in Islam entails supporting one another during life's storms and celebrating together when the sun shines again. The garden became a living testament to the beauty of friendship, reminding the community that true friendship bonds are like resilient plants, capable of thriving even in the face of adversity.

So, in the tight-knit neighbourhood where laughter echoed through the streets, Tahir's story became a reminder that friendships, nurtured through shared experiences and cultivated with care, are among the most valuable treasures one can have in life.

VALUE 25: FRIENDSHIP

VALUE 26: KNOWLEDGE SEEKING

NORA'S QUEST FOR KNOWLEDGE

A girl named Nora lived in a town where the stars whispered secrets to the moon and the books in the library held tales of endless possibilities. Nora had a curious heart and eyes that sparkled with curiosity. Nora felt a gentle tug on her spirit one sunny day as she walked past the library - a call to embark on a Quest for Knowledge.

Nora entered the library, a treasure trove of books just waiting to be discovered. She decided to seek knowledge that would spark her imagination and help her grow with a twinkle in her eye.

Her first stop was in the animal section. Nora read books about animals large and small, from elephants with swinging trunks to ants who build tiny kingdoms. She marvelled at the animal kingdom's diversity, realising that each creature held a lesson about the wonders of life.

Nora then descended into the realm of numbers and shapes. She flipped through pages of colourful equations and geometric marvels. She felt the joy of unlocking the secrets of mathematics with each discovery, realising that numbers were more than symbols - they were the language of the universe.

Her journey continued through the history books, where she learned about ancient civilizations and brave explorers. Nora had the impression that she was travelling through time, absorbing lessons from the past and gaining wisdom to guide her into the future.

Nora's understanding of the world grew as she read about different cultures. She discovered that diversity was a treasure, and that knowledge was the key to unlocking empathy and connecting people.

Nora's world grew larger as she sought knowledge. The library transformed into her magical realm, and each book opened the door to a new adventure. Nora felt empowered and excited with each page turn, realising that the quest for knowledge was a lifelong journey full of endless discoveries.

The story of Nora's Quest for Knowledge quickly spread throughout the town, and other children soon joined her in the library. The quiet area was transformed into a hive of activity, with children eagerly flipping through books, their eyes wide with delight at the prospect of learning.

The town grew into a community of knowledge seekers as Nora shared her discoveries with her friends. The wonders of science, the beauty of language, and the power of ideas were all taught to children. Nora's quest had piqued the interest of everyone who had followed her lead.

Nora's Quest for Knowledge became a legendary tale in the town where the stars whispered secrets to the moon and the books in the library held tales of endless possibilities. The story resonated in the hearts of children, inspiring them to value education, seek useful knowledge, and embark on their own journeys of discovery.

VALUE 27: PURITY OF HEART

ZAYN'S PURE HEART

A boy named Zayn lived in a town where the flowers bloomed with kindness and the birds whispered stories of affection. Zayn had a pure heart as clear as a stream and eyes that saw the beauty in everyone.

Yasir and Amin, Zayn's friends, were excitedly talking about Yasir's beautiful kite soaring high in the sky. Instead of sharing their joy, Zayn's heart was filled with jealousy. He wished he had a kite like that, and the green monster of envy cast a cloud over his cheerful demeanour.

A wise old woman approached Zayn as he walked away. "Zayn, a pure heart is like a garden full of flowers," she said with a twinkle in her eye. "Jealousy and negativity, however, have the potential to ruin even the most beautiful blossoms."

Zayn questioned the wise woman about how to keep his heart pure. "Love for others what you love for yourself". Keep this thought close to you and allow it to serve as a reminder to cultivate love, sincerity, and purity in your heart."

Zayn returned to his friends with this in mind. Instead of being envious, he cheered as Yasir's kite danced in the sky. This sensation warmed Zayn's heart, and he felt light and free.

The following day, Zayn faced a new challenge. Amin showed him his beautifully painted picture, and an emotion of envy crept into his heart once more. Zayn expressed his heartfelt congratulations to Amin, recalling the wise woman's words. His heart, which had once been clouded by jealousy, now shone with the purity of kindness.

Zayn's heart changed as time passed. It served as a guide, reminding him to celebrate the success of others and to see the beauty in their accomplishments. His friendships blossomed, and the once-jealous feelings faded, leaving a garden of love and sincerity in their place.

So, in the town where the flowers bloomed with kindness and the butterflies whispered love stories, the story echoed through the hearts of children, inspiring them to cultivate love, sincerity, and purity of heart in their relationships, ensuring that the gardens of their hearts were always filled with the most beautiful blossoms.

VALUE 28: DUA

ZEESHAN'S PRAYER BEADS

In a town where the wind carried whispers of hope and the stars twinkled like tiny lanterns, there lived a boy named Zeeshan. Zeeshan had a heart as gentle as a moonlit night and eyes that sparkled with curiosity. One day, as he strolled through the market, he stumbled upon a small shop with a sign that read, "Special Prayer Beads."

Intrigued, Zeeshan entered the shop where an old man with a kind smile greeted him. The old man explained that these prayer beads held the wonders of Dhikr and Dua (remembrance and supplication). Zeeshan, with a heart full of wonder, purchased a prayer bead.

That evening, as Zeeshan held the beads in his hands, he wondered about their special powers. The old man had told him that each bead held the power to turn his thoughts into prayers, connecting him directly to Allah. Excitedly, Zeeshan decided to try it out.

He held the first bead and whispered a prayer for his family's well-being. As he moved to the next bead, he asked Allah for success in his studies. With each bead, Zeeshan poured his heart out to Allah, sharing his hopes, fears, and dreams.

To his amazement, as Zeeshan finished his prayers, he felt a warmth in his heart. The duas he made to Allah had transformed his worries into words of supplication, and he felt a sense of peace that he had never experienced before.

From that day on, Zeeshan made it a habit to use his prayer beads as an aid to make dua regularly. When he faced challenges at school, he turned to Allah for guidance. When he felt sad, he sought comfort in the loving words of his Creator. The beads became a bridge between Zeeshan and Allah, a gripping connection that filled his heart with gratitude and trust.

Word of Zeeshan's prayer beads spread through the town, and soon, other children visited the shop to get their own. The old man, pleased with the impact of the beads, shared a secret with each child – the real magic wasn't in the beads but in the sincerity of their duas.

Zeeshan, now a source of inspiration, organized a prayer circle in the town's park. Children sat together, sharing their hopes and dreams with Allah. The park became a place of serenity and unity, as the children discovered the power of Dua in bringing people closer to each other and to Allah.

And so, in the town where the wind carried whispers of hope and the stars twinkled like tiny lanterns, the story echoed through the hearts of children, inspiring them to develop a habit of Dua, turning to Allah in all situations and trusting in the magic of heartfelt supplication.

VALUE 29: GRACIOUSNESS

HIBA'S ACT OF GRACE

A girl named Hiba lived in a town where the sun painted the sky with warm hues and the flowers whispered secrets of kindness. Hiba's heart was as gentle as a butterfly's touch, and her eyes sparkled with compassion. As she skipped through the park one day, she came across an opportunity to weave a story of grace.

Mrs. Johnson, an elderly neighbour, was struggling to carry groceries into her house when Hiba noticed her. "Let me help, Mrs. Johnson!" Hiba rushed to her side without hesitation.

Mrs. Johnson handed Hiba a bag with a grateful smile. Hiba, however, did not stop at the door and instead followed Mrs. Johnson inside. Mrs. Johnson, surprised, asked, "Oh dear, you've done enough." You are welcome to leave the bags here."

But Hiba, with a kind heart, insisted on organising the groceries in the kitchen. Mrs. Johnson watched in awe as Hiba went above and beyond, neatly placing items on shelves and ensuring everything was in order.

Mrs. Johnson could feel grace filling the room as Hiba worked. It wasn't just about carrying groceries; it was about Hiba's genuine concern and effort to make a difference.

Hiba smiled brightly at Mrs. Johnson once everything was in place. "There you go, all set!"

Mrs. Johnson, moved by Hiba's act of kindness, couldn't help but express her gratitude. "Thank you very much, dear. You've transformed a simple task into a lovely act of kindness."

Hiba's Act of Grace spread throughout the neighbourhood, and other children were soon inspired to do the same. The park became a space for thoughtful gestures ranging from chore assistance to the sharing of toys and laughter.

A group of children approached Hiba while she was playing in the park one day. They said, "We want to be like you, Hiba!"

Hiba gathered the children and revealed her secret, "Graciousness is about going the extra mile, doing more than what's expected." The smallest details make a big difference."

The children committed to performing acts of kindness throughout the town as a group. They assisted neighbours with garden work, painted encouraging messages on rocks and even planned a surprise picnic for the elderly residents.

So, in the town where the sun painted the sky with warm hues and the flowers whispered kindness secrets, the story echoed through the hearts of children, inspiring them to discover the beauty of going beyond expectations, one kind act at a time.

VALUE 29: GRACIOUSNESS

VALUE 30: TOLERANCE

LINA'S CULTURAL ACCEPTANCE

Lina, a curious girl, lived in a vibrant community where the echoes of different languages and the colours of various cultures painted the neighbourhood. Lina had always been fascinated by the unique traditions and stories brought by her friends and neighbours from their respective backgrounds. She had no idea that a special event was about to take place that would teach her the profound Islamic value of acceptance and appreciation for the rich diversity of cultures.

The community decided to hold a Cultural Exchange Fair one day. Families were encouraged to share their customs, traditions, and cuisines. Lina decided to explore the fair with an open heart and mind because she was excited about the opportunity to learn.

Lina encountered a plethora of colours, sounds, and flavours as she strolled through the fair. Each booth represented a different culture, providing a glimpse into the community's rich diversity. Lina listened to folk tales and ate delectable dishes from around the world.

Lina, on the other hand, noticed apprehension among some attendees. Some people were hesitant to embrace customs that were different from their own. Lina decided to create a "Bridge of Understanding" display at the fair in order to bridge this gap. She asked everyone to bring something that represented their culture, such as a photo, a symbol, or even a treasured family recipe.

The response was heartfelt. Families eagerly shared their cultural treasures, and the Bridge of Understanding quickly transformed into a visual tapestry, intertwining the threads of diverse backgrounds into a harmonious whole.

Lina realised the profound Islamic value of acceptance as she admired the display. Islam encourages believers to value and respect cultural diversity, recognising it as a manifestation of Allah's creative design. Lina's efforts to build a bridge of understanding echoed Islamic teachings of unity and appreciation.

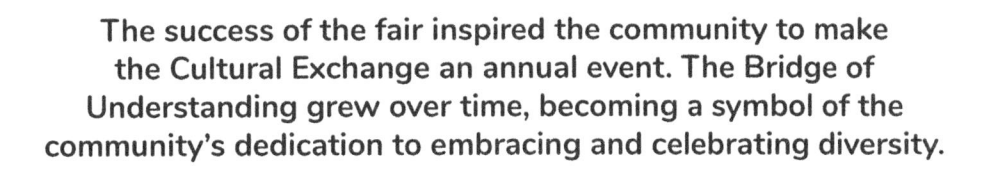

The success of the fair inspired the community to make the Cultural Exchange an annual event. The Bridge of Understanding grew over time, becoming a symbol of the community's dedication to embracing and celebrating diversity.

Lina learned from this experience that the beauty of Islam lies in accepting and understanding others. The more we value the rich tapestry of cultures that surround us, the closer we will be to embodying the true spirit of Islam—uniting people in a bond of humanity that transcends borders and differences.

Lina's story became a beacon of acceptance in the vibrant community where the echoes of different languages and the colours of diverse cultures painted the neighbourhood, reminding everyone that the tapestry of humanity is woven with threads of various hues, each contributing to the splendid canvas of life.

Made in the USA
Coppell, TX
13 July 2024